JUGS

R. K. Henrywood

SHIRE PUBLICATIONS

Published in Great Britain in 2009 by Shire Publications Ltd, Midland House, West Way, Botley, Oxford OX2 0PH, United Kingdom.

443 Park Avenue South, New York, NY 10016, USA.

E-mail: shire@shirebooks.co.uk   www.shirebooks.co.uk

A CIP catalogue record for this book is available from the British Library.

Shire Library no. 287   •   ISBN-13: 978 0 74780 734 6

R. K. Henrywood has asserted his right under the Copyright, Designs and Patents Act, 1988, to be identified as the author of this book.

Designed by Ken Vail Graphic Design, Cambridge, UK and typeset in Perpetua and Gill Sans.

Printed in Malta by Gutenberg Press Ltd.

09 10 11 12 13   10 9 8 7 6 5 4 3 2 1

COVER IMAGE
(Back rows) Buff stoneware jug moulded with Tam O'Shanter characters, maker unknown, c. 1830; brown saltware-glazed stoneware jug with applied motto, Doulton, c. 1890; white stoneware jug moulded with David and Goliath scenes, Thomas Till, c. 1854; blue-printed jug decorated with 'views in Wales', probably Welsh, c. 1840; blue-printed jug with one of a series of rural scenes, maker unknown, c. 1825. (Front rows) Lavendar and white Parian jug moulded with a scene from the battle of Acre, Samuel Alcock and Company, c. 1845; typical ironstone jug with a colourful Japan pattern, Masons, c. 1820; small stoneware jug with white sprigs, maker unknown, c. 1825; miniature moulded jug with a scene from 'Paul and Virginia', T. J. & J Mayer, c. 1850; blue stoneware jug sprigged with Classical scenes, maker unknown, c. 1820.

TITLE PAGE IMAGE
A large earthenware dealer's display jug, colourfully painted with flowers by William Fifield at Bristol, signed and dated August 1824.

CONTENTS PAGE IMAGE
Four very typical jugs by the prolific William Brownfield firm, these titled 'Donatello' (registered in 1861), 'Tyrol' (1864), 'Cupid' (1872) and 'Yeddo' (1876). Brownfield issued many designs, usually titled, and most made in plain stoneware, with coloured backgrounds or with more extensive colouring.

ACKNOWLEDGEMENTS
Anderson & Garland, page 40 (left); Author, pages 10, 12 (top right, bottom left), 13, 14, 15 (top, centre), and 38 (top left); Bamfords, pages 9, 16, 26 (top right), and 41 (left); Bearnes, pages 37 (left), and 48 (bottom left); Paul Beighton, page 38 (bottom right); Bonhams, pages 26 (top left), and 52 (bottom right); Bonningtons, page 44 (top left); Byrne's, page 19 (right); Charterhouse, page 45 (bottom left); Chilcotts, page 51 (top); Dreweatt Neate, pages 1, 3, 12 (top left), 15 (bottom), 19 (left), 20, 21 (left), 22–4, 26 (bottom), 27–31, 34 (bottom), 35 (top right), 36 (top left), 39 (top and bottom), 44 (top right, bottom), 46 (top), and 48 (bottom right); Duke's, page 12 (bottom right); Fieldings, pages 49, and 50 (top); Gorringes, pages 18 (top left), and 40 (right); Green Valley Auctions, page 21 (right); Hansons, page 53 (bottom right); Hutchinson Scott, page 38 (top right, bottom left); Jones & Jacob, page 45 (bottom right); Keys, Aylsham, pages 51 (bottom left), 52 (top, bottom left), and 53; Mallams, Cheltenham, page 39 (centre left); Thomas Mawer, page 35 (centre); Mellors & Kirk, pages 18 (bottom), 34 (top left, top right), 36 (top right), 37 (right), 42, 45 (top right), and 47 (bottom); Phillips, page 8 (left); Private collection, page 18 (top right); Rosebery's, page 39 (centre right); Sotheby's, pages 4, 6, and 7; Sworders, pages 8 (right), 32, and 48 (top); Tennants, pages 36 (centre), and 47 (top); Woolley & Wallis, pages 35 (top left, bottom), 41 (right), 45 (top left), 46 (bottom), and 50 (bottom).

Shire Publications is supporting the Woodland Trust, the UK's leading woodland conservation charity, by funding the dedication of trees.

CONTENTS

INTRODUCTION

O NE OF THE QUIRKS of modern life is that our use of jugs for serving anything other than milk and cream has all but disappeared. We are so used to the convenience of modern supermarkets that we often forget the earlier days when there were no plastic bottles, no cardboard containers, no tins and few glass vessels. Liquids still had to be fetched, stored and served, and the only widely available vessel would be the simple pottery jug.

In the nineteenth century in particular, jugs were used for staples such as water and milk, a tremendous variety of alcoholic beverages including beer and cider, and some almost forgotten drinks such as porter and toddy. Since most households would need several jugs, a mass market developed, and there was great competition among the potters. Despite their utilitarian function, decorative jugs sold much more readily, and a vast number of attractive designs were produced. Such jugs have survived in large numbers and since they are very easy to display, either singly or as collections, they are particularly popular with collectors.

Pottery vessels designed to hold and serve liquids have been made since prehistoric times. The earliest jugs were very crude, fashioned by hand in poor-quality earthenware, but towards the end of the seventeenth century more sophisticated wares began to appear. Although the body was still quite poor, this was covered with various forms of glaze, particularly a white glaze based on tin, often referred to as delftware after the Dutch town where similar-looking pots originated. These wares were made in various pottery centres in England, including London, Bristol and Liverpool, and were usually decorated with designs hand-painted in blue although a manganese purple and other techniques were sometimes used.

Another form of decoration surviving from earlier times was the use of coloured clays or slip to cover the body. Such slipwares tend to be well known by virtue of a number of famous large chargers signed, and sometimes dated, by the potter, but jugs were also made, again sometimes dated. A shiny black glaze was also developed in the eighteenth century, normally referred to as

Finely painted and gilt jug attributed to Spode, c. 1815. Porcelain and china jugs are often beautifully decorated by hand, but they were expensive and heavily outnumbered by utilitarian jugs in earthenware or stoneware.

Above: Five typical medieval jugs; most of these were made in the Nottingham area between the eleventh and fifteenth centuries.

Right: A fine Staffordshire slipware jug with slip-trailed decoration in brown and cream, initialled and dated 1704 around the rim.

Jackfield ware after the Shropshire village, although most examples were probably made in Staffordshire.

Another early body was salt-glazed stoneware, originally coarse and coloured brown but later made of a finer white clay. The brown wares were strong but crude, but the white wares could be surprisingly sophisticated, and some are also finely decorated. From the beginning of the eighteenth century jugs were also made from fine red clays, some of which were highly fired to make red stoneware. Porcelain made its appearance in the middle of the century and was used for high-quality jugs, but they were very expensive and out of reach for the general public.

It was the various finer earthenware and stoneware bodies that were to become the norm for utilitarian jugs. The first really successful body was creamware, so called after its cream-coloured glaze, which provided a good

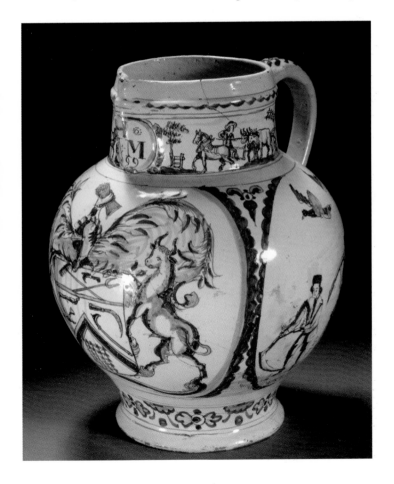

A London tin-glazed earthenware or delftware harvest jug painted in blue with the Farmers' arms, initialled and dated 1699 beneath the spout.

smooth surface suitable for decoration, initially painting but soon transfer printing. Creamware was made into the early nineteenth century, although by then it had largely been superseded by pearlware, with a much whiter glaze. They developed into a good utilitarian earthenware that was to become the backbone of many potteries' output.

Other eighteenth-century bodies included black basalt, jasper wares and caneware, all forms of stoneware, and a semi-translucent body known as felspathic stoneware. For various reasons, none of these proved entirely successful for everyday jugs subjected to heavy usage; some were too expensive, others insufficiently durable. A major breakthrough was achieved by John Turner of Lane End, who developed a fine white body that was to form the basis of most stonewares used through the nineteenth century.

These earthenwares and stonewares were joined in the early nineteenth century by 'stone china', developed separately by John Turner of Lane End and Josiah Spode of Stoke, but also by the Mason firm, which stole a march on its rivals by coining the trade name 'Patent Ironstone China'. The use of the word 'china' is misleading since stone china is actually a form of stoneware, but the term was clearly adopted as a marketing ploy and proved hugely successful. Many other potters went on to develop similar bodies under a host of different trade names, but they are all similar and were widely used for utilitarian jugs.

Below:
A Staffordshire red stoneware jug decorated with cream sprigs including the royal coat of arms, c. 1740–50.

Below right:
A mid-eighteenth-century creamware jug of Whieldon type, with a mask spout, covered overall with a tortoiseshell glaze.

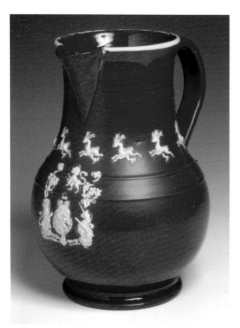

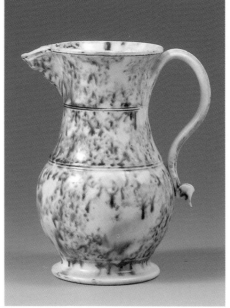

A fine eighteenth-century presentation creamware jug hand-painted in underglaze blue with a detailed view of Thomas Newcomen's steam or 'fire' engine, inscribed 'S. Tompson' but not dated, c. 1780.

Jugs from the eighteenth century have survived in reasonable numbers, and many superb examples can be seen in museum collections. Later examples, particularly those from Victorian times, are still very widely available and form the basis of many private collections. The most common types are those with sprigged, transfer-printed or relief-moulded decoration, and each of these decorative techniques is described in more detail below.

No short survey of this type could hope to achieve any more than a general introduction to the jugs that have been such an important product for pottery manufacturers through the ages. Jugs were made in virtually every material used by the potters, and any reader seeking more detail can find much more information in reference books intended primarily for collectors, an excellent example of which is Griselda Lewis's *A Collector's History of English Pottery*.

SPRIG MOULDING

T HE USE OF MOULDS in the manufacture of pottery goes back to ancient times, but the mass production of moulded wares did not become a practical proposition until the discovery of plaster of Paris. Earlier moulds were made of wood, alabaster, or sometimes fired clay itself. Even brass was used for some very small designs. None of these materials was ideal: they were either too coarse, too difficult to work, too expensive or, more seriously, not sufficiently absorbent. Absorbency was crucial for mass production, and the introduction of plaster of Paris to the Staffordshire Potteries, traditionally attributed to Ralph Daniel in 1746, was an important turning point. In addition to its absorbency, which helped to dry the clay in the mould, plaster of Paris was capable of reproducing extremely fine detail.

Although plaster of Paris moulds were later to be used for casting complete jugs in one process, their earliest use was for a technique known as sprig moulding. Moulds were made to cast small flat pieces of clay, rather like cameos in jewellery, which were then attached to the surface of a pot using liquid clay, known as slip. The main vessel itself could still be made by traditional means such as turning on the potter's wheel.

Sprig decoration of this type can still be seen on today's popular blue and white Wedgwood jasper ware, but back in the second half of the eighteenth century the technique was very widely adopted. Examples can be found on jugs made in many different materials, notably stoneware-type bodies such as caneware, black basalt and jasper. Sprig moulds were not so suitable for the coarser-bodied earthenwares, but they proved particularly successful on the fine-bodied white stoneware, traditionally invented by John Turner of Lane End. He made some magnificent jugs with sprigged decoration, featuring mainly Classical figures, but sometimes also scenes from contemporary life such as an archery lesson.

Jugs in fine white stoneware of this type were made by several other manufacturers, including particularly Adams and Hollins, and, despite changes of fashion, they continued in production well into the nineteenth century. The later examples were made by Spode, Davenport, Wedgwood

Opposite:
A good-quality jug by David Wilson of Hanley, c. 1810–15, the chocolate-brown body sprigged in white; variations of this hunting scene were adopted by many other potters.

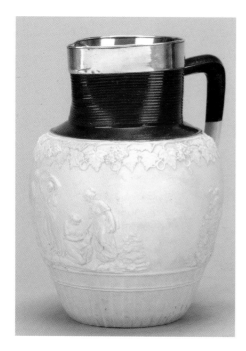

Left: A typical sprigged stoneware jug by John Turner of Lane End, c. 1790–1800. This example is decorated with classical figures, although Turner used a range of different designs; the metal rim is plated, but hallmarked silver rims are occasionally found.

Above: Another white stoneware jug, this example by Benjamin Adams of Tunstall, c. 1800–10. Several other firms made similar jugs at this period.

Below: A distinctive jug with a chocolate brown body made by Samuel Hollins at Shelton, c. 1790–1800. In addition to using coloured bodies, Hollins experimented with a process similar to electroplating to apply metallic finishes – different from silver lustre, which came slightly later.

A marked Brameld drab stoneware jug sprig-decorated with classical cherubs, the handle in the form of a horse's tail and hoof.

and others. One common design shows a group of huntsmen at the kill, and this was produced by several Staffordshire potters, probably, in the case of the smaller firms, from widely available moulds supplied by specialist mould makers. Some examples of this and many other patterns are found embellished with a coloured ground behind the sprigs, usually blue or brown, although other colours were used.

The main development in sprigged ware was the introduction of coloured bodies. It is not surprising that the impressive contrast of white sprigs on a coloured body, or less commonly coloured sprigs on a white body, was to prove popular. Wares of this type appeared at the end of the eighteenth century and were subsequently produced in quantity, particularly by Ridgway, but also by Spode and Wedgwood and several smaller firms including David Wilson, Ralph & James Clews, and a host of unidentified potters. Examples clearly marked with the potter's name are occasionally found, but many are unmarked.

Some unidentified makers used small 'pad' marks, moulded separately and applied with liquid slip like the sprigged decoration itself. These pad marks, mostly dating between about 1815 and 1835, are of various forms, but the only one to be positively identified is of a lozenge shape and was used by one of the Ridgway firms. Most of them feature no identification except

Another coloured-body jug decorated with white sprigs. This example, by Ridgway c. 1815–25, is marked with one of the popular pad marks containing a model number, in this case 269.

Top left: A small jug with blue sprigs on a white body, c. 1815–30. The unknown maker of this jug used a small rectangular pad mark, this example with model number 115.

Top right: Another jug by an unknown maker marked with a model number, in this case number 31, allied to a trade name 'Imperial Stone', c. 1820–30. Note the moulded body, which marks a transitional phase between sprigged wares and fully moulded jugs.

Bottom left: An octagonal jug of common 'Hydra' shape in white china decorated with lavender floral and classical sprigs. This design can also be found in stoneware, usually grey, and most examples bear an impressed name 'ORIENTAL'.

Bottom right: A later jug from a series marked 'Milan', probably made by Dudson of Hanley, c. 1870. These 'Milan'-shape jugs come in various bodies, but the use of terracotta with basalt sprigs is unusual.

a model number, although one, found on a range of sprigged stonewares, includes the trade name 'Imperial Stone'. Other forms of mark were used, including impressed names such as 'Oriental' and 'Milan'. The first of these is found on octagonal jugs, usually made of grey stoneware but sometimes of white china, whereas the other appears on a range of jugs of a fairly distinctive shape, possibly made by Dudson around 1860–70.

Sprig decoration was mostly superseded by fully moulded wares from about 1830 or so, but some firms continued to produce high-quality sprigged jugs. Wedgwood specialised in the technique and it was also retained by Copelands, who succeeded Spode and continued to make high-quality sprigged wares into the twenty-first century. James Dudson, one of a family

of Staffordshire potters, made a speciality of sprigged jugs in the second half of the nineteenth century. These are usually of a simple tankard shape and can be found in various colours and with a very wide range of sprigged designs. Many of these can be traced back to the early wares made by Wedgwood, Turner and others, and it is important to note that, except in a few unusual cases, it is not normally safe to attribute unmarked wares on the basis of sprig designs alone.

An impressive blue stoneware jug by an unknown maker dubbed the 'Chrysanthemum Factory', c. 1815–25. The name derives from the chrysanthemum-shaped pad mark used to contain a model number, in this case 5.

Left:
A set of three tankard-shaped jugs by Dudson of Hanley, c. 1870–80. Dudson made a very large number of jugs at this period using a wide variety of sprig designs, different colours and various shapes, of which this is the most common.

Left: Two Copeland jugs in off-white stoneware with a blue ground; late nineteenth or early twentieth century. The sprigged scene on the right can be traced back nearly one hundred years earlier to the Herculaneum Pottery at Liverpool.

MATRIMONY

That form once o'er with anger strew,
The Married pair both prettily & loud;
All night and day they scold & fight,
She calls him ass & he calls her fool.

COURTSHIP

When two fond fools together meet,
Each look gives joy each kiss so sweet;
But Wed how cold and cross they be.
Turn up side down and then you'll see.

TRANSFER PRINTING

W HILE SPRIG MOULDING was a popular technique for decorating various types of stoneware bodies used for jugs in the second half of the eighteenth century, a completely parallel development was the use of transfer printing on earthenwares. The first successful use of the technique was achieved by the Liverpool printers John Sadler and Guy Green. They petitioned for a patent for their process in 1756, claiming that they had printed more than twelve hundred tiles in six hours, which were 'more in number, and better, and neater than one hundred skilful pot painters could have painted'.

Sadler and Green came to an arrangement with Wedgwood to decorate his creamwares with printed patterns, usually in black but sometimes purple, and these early examples can be of exceptionally high quality. Other potters and printers used the same process, but it did suffer from the drawback that the prints were applied over the glaze and, despite being fixed with an additional firing, the decoration could slowly fade or wear away if the pots were subject to frequent use. This problem could best be overcome by printing under the glaze, and this was to be the logical next development.

The invention of blue and white underglaze printing on pottery is traditionally attributed to Thomas Turner at Caughley, but early marked wares of this type were made by John Turner at Lane End, by Josiah Spode at Stoke, and by a lesser-known potter with the initials I. H., probably John Harrison of Stoke. From about 1790 onwards printing was to develop into a major industry, and throughout the nineteenth century vast quantities of printed ware were produced by virtually all potteries involved in making utilitarian pottery. The technique was particularly applied to dinner services, but every item imaginable was made, including some very rare shapes, ranging from small asparagus servers to very large footbaths and even smoker's companions.

Blue-printed jugs are common and examples can be found from most of the well-known manufacturers, such as Spode, Minton, Ridgway and Wedgwood. Some manufacturers seem to have specialised in printed wares,

Opposite:
A late-eighteenth-century creamware jug, possibly made in Liverpool, printed in black with an amusing design showing a couple in good humour during courtship, but when the jug is inverted they are at loggerheads after matrimony; the reverse has a country scene.

Above left: Nautical subjects were popular, and this design, titled 'Susan's Farewell', shows a woman waving a fond farewell to her sailor boy, c. 1800. The sailor's farewell and return were common themes on jugs, including later examples from Sunderland, where they were also widely used on wall plaques.

Above: A wash jug or ewer, printed with a rural scene in black with hand-coloured highlights, c. 1810–20. This style of decoration, with the basic print in either black or brown, is more often found on tea wares. This wash-jug shape remained popular throughout the nineteenth century.

Above: A blue-printed jug commemorating the death of Admiral Lord Nelson at the Battle of Trafalgar in 1805. The use of ochre lining on the rim and handle was quite common at this period.

particularly John Rogers & Son of Longport, William Adams of Stoke, Ralph & James Clews of Cobridge, and Enoch Wood & Sons of Burslem. The list of manufacturers is extensive, and wares were produced not only in Staffordshire but also in the other major pottery districts of Bristol, South Wales, Liverpool, Yorkshire, Sunderland, Tyneside and Scotland. Much detailed information can be found in the two volumes of *The Dictionary of Blue and White Printed Pottery 1780–1880* by A. W. Coysh and R. K. Henrywood.

As with blue-printed wares in general, an enormous range of patterns was used to decorate jugs. In the early years, from 1780 through to about 1810, designs were predominantly in the chinoiserie style. The common 'Willow' pattern, an entirely imaginary scene with a pagoda, three figures on a bridge, an island, a boat and two doves, evolved during this period and was to become a standard design produced by very many nineteenth-century potters.

From about 1810 scenic patterns began to appear, initially overseas views from places such as India and Italy, but soon including numerous British, European and American scenes. Virtually all of these were based on engravings in books of the period, blatantly copied by the potters until the Copyright Act of 1842 attempted to prevent such piracy. Some very good botanical and floral patterns were made in the period 1810 to 1830, although later designs of this type became less and less distinguished.

After the mid 1830s engravers tended to concentrate on either wholly imaginary scenes or floral designs, generally printed in a lighter blue than the earlier patterns. The imaginary scenes tend to follow a formula, with a

Above left:
A wash jug printed in blue with an early chinoiserie scene known to collectors as the 'Two Figures' pattern. This is a typical early design, line-engraved and printed in a dark steely blue with little gradation of tone, c. 1790.

Above: Another chinoiserie jug, inscribed and dated 'Matthew & Hannah Tym, 1805'. Chinoiserie patterns like this were being superseded from about this time although the standard 'Willow' pattern was to remain in production throughout the nineteenth century.

Above:
A view of Orielton in Pembrokeshire on a jug by John & Richard Riley of Burslem, one of a series of views copied from a book of engravings by John Preston Neale. Views of country houses were popular on blue-printed wares in the 1820s and early 1830s.

Above right:
A Dutch-shape jug from around 1820 decorated with an attractive print of a woman spinning wool while two companions stand watching. Many genre scenes were produced in the 1815–35 period, mostly unmarked and by unknown makers.

Another Dutch-shape jug, this example by Minton in the factory's semi-china 'Floral Vases' pattern, c. 1830. Jugs with covers are normally fitted with a strainer behind the spout and are often called 'toast-water jugs', reflecting their use for serving a supposedly beneficial liquid to invalids.

river or lake, a building such as a castle or classical temple, mountains in the background, a tree overhanging from one side, and a feature such as a group of people, a fountain or a vase in the foreground. They are generally referred to as 'romantic' patterns and, although they often bear titles such as 'Andalusia', 'Corinth', 'Dacca', 'Delaware', 'Milan', 'Rhine' or 'Sicilian', the pictures bear little relation, if any, to the places named.

Earlier printed wares are usually unmarked but some examples bear simple impressed marks, easy to apply on flatwares but more difficult on open wares such as jugs, which were not suited for the pressure necessary to impress the mark. Where jugs are found with an impressed mark, it is almost invariably very close to or even actually on the foot-rim.

One of the advantages of printed decoration was the greater ease with which pieces could be marked. The engraver would include the mark on the same copper plate as the main pattern and, when the transfer was applied, it was an easy matter to cut the mark from the transfer tissue and apply it to the bottom of the piece. As printed marks became widespread they quickly became more ornate and informative. Marks often include the maker's name, sometimes an address, a pattern title, a trade name such as 'Opaque China' or 'Improved Stone Ware', and any one of a range of decorative features such as garters, crowns, coats of arms and, later in the nineteenth century, trademarks. However, although printed marks are much more common than the earlier impressed marks, a significant number of jugs are unmarked, and detective work is often needed to come up with satisfactory attributions.

Below left:
A pearlware jug printed in brown and picked out with underglaze Pratt colours, probably made at Ferrybridge in Yorkshire, c. 1800. Printing in other than blue was uncommon before 1825, and particularly so at this early period.

Below:
A 'Lake Scenery' pattern jug in brown and red by Enoch Wood & Sons of Burslem, c. 1830–5. Two-colour prints like this are uncommon in Britain and were made largely for export to the United States, where they are eagerly collected.

Blue was the first colour used for underglaze printing since initially the potters were unable to make any other ink capable of withstanding the heat necessary to fix the glaze. Some early wares are found in other colours, particularly brown or black, sometimes enhanced by other colouring such as underglaze Pratt-type colours, but blue was dominant until about 1830. By this time the earlier technical problems had been overcome, and printed jugs can be found in black, grey, brown, green, rarely yellow, but many shades of pink, red and purple. These later colours are not particularly common in Britain, and they were probably made predominantly for export to North America. Some potters printed in two colours on the same piece, and these items can be most attractive and are very collectable. As a general rule, colours other than blue have not achieved great popularity in Britain and, although the wares from the 1830s onwards are not as interesting as those from the earlier years, this could be a rewarding field for further study.

One other technique is known as 'flow-blue'. The process is just the same as for normal printing, but when the final firing takes place a chemical is introduced into the kiln that encourages the ink to flow into the glaze, thus producing a rather smudged or blurred appearance. Flow-blue wares appear to have been made mostly for export to America and they are not widely found in Britain. The patterns are usually floral or geometric in nature, or romantic-style chinoiserie. The same technique was used with a greyish-purple colour, known as 'flow-mulberry', again made for export. These 'flown' wares have some enthusiastic collectors but are considered unattractive by many others.

Below:
A jug printed in green, picked out in enamels, with a design titled 'Country Sports', by Elijah Jones of Cobridge, c. 1835. Note the ornate, Rococo-style shape, typical of the 1830s and 1840s.

Below right:
A fine and large dairy jug with a scroll-moulded body printed in black with a 'Dresden Opaque China' design of floral sprays, c. 1830. Note the extra support fitted on the front of the jug – a large jug full of milk would be very heavy.

A 'Whampoa' pattern jug by Dillwyn & Company of Swansea, c. 1840–50. Flow-blue wares, with the print chemically 'flown' in the kiln, typically featuring romantic chinoiserie designs, are both loved and loathed by different collectors.

A jug by an unknown maker, printed in colour with a scene of birds and flowers, c. 1860. Multicolour printing, particularly associated with pot-lids and the Pratt and Mayer firms, was not widely used on jugs, the technique being difficult to apply to curved surfaces.

Multicoloured printing made its first appearance in the late 1830s with some attractive wares made at the Davenport factory, but the technique was particularly developed by F. & R. Pratt & Company, so much so that such wares have become known as Prattwares, not to be confused with earlier moulded and underglaze-painted wares to be discussed briefly in the next section. While the Pratt firm specialised in pot-lids, they also made many other attractive useful wares. Other firms made similar products, particularly T. J. & J. Mayer of Longport, but also several smaller potters. Jugs are relatively uncommon since the technique did not lend itself well to application on doubly curved surfaces.

While printed wares in plain colours were made throughout the nineteenth century, later jugs often have added decoration in the form of coloured backgrounds, overglaze enamels or added lustre, or even, in some cases, relatively expensive gilding. Although transfer-printing declined in importance from the 1880s onwards, it never died out and is still widely used today.

RELIEF MOULDING

ALTHOUGH SPRIG MOULDING survived throughout the nineteenth century, the manufacture of sprigged wares required considerable skill. The potters were clearly motivated to compete by reducing the cost of their products, and one way to achieve this was to use less skilled labour. An obvious advance was to use moulds to produce the complete jug, not just for sprigs applied to decorate the surface. Fully moulded jugs had been made as early as 1750, but this method was not very successful with the white salt-glazed stoneware body then in use.

Moulded jugs were also made in quantity at the end of the eighteenth century and into the early nineteenth, this time made of pearlware or other similar earthenwares that needed to be glazed. Many of these jugs were coloured underglaze with a typical palette including shades of green, blue and orange. These jugs are known generically as Prattwares, although they were made by many potters other than Pratt. Although they were popular and successful in their way, the glazed earthenware body was not without its problems, and by about 1820 the potters began to manufacture fully moulded jugs made of fine-bodied stoneware. These jugs represent the culmination of developments bringing together the use of plaster moulds and the fine stoneware body originated by John Turner. Although this body was initially developed for its whiteness, when the moulded jugs emerged the potters almost immediately used stains to produce attractive coloured wares, initially drab or buff, but soon also pastel shades of green and blue, in addition to plain white.

The earliest jug of this type appears to be a hunting scene made by Phillips & Bagster, who were potting in Hanley between about 1818 and 1823, but by the mid 1830s several major makers had adopted the process. Among these were William Ridgway of Hanley and Herbert Minton of Stoke, both of whom made many attractive and collectable jugs. They were soon joined by Charles Meigh of Hanley, who made some particularly notable Gothic and Classical designs, and also by Elijah Jones and Edward Walley of Cobridge, who, while little known for other wares, made some notable jugs, both individually and in partnership.

Opposite:
A popular jug by Charles Meigh of Hanley, titled 'York Minster Jug' and registered in 1846. The reverse shows a similar group of Mary and Jesus with St John the Baptist.

25

Above left:
A typical early nineteenth-century Prattware jug, moulded and picked out with underglaze colours. Prattwares are usually unmarked, but this example is impressed 'STEVENSON', probably made by one of the Stevenson family firms at Cobridge in Staffordshire.

Above:
A Prattware jug, c. 1810–20, and typically unmarked, decorated with heart-shaped panels with scenes titled 'Mischievous Sport' (shown) and 'Sportive Innocence' (on the reverse).

Two Meigh jugs, these known as the 'Four Seasons', registered by Charles Meigh & Son in 1852, and 'Amphitrite', after the Greek sea goddess, registered in 1856. The use of a coloured background, particularly blue, became popular from the 1840s.

A fine set of four jugs by Samuel Alcock & Company in a 'Camel' pattern, originally available with lavender or blue colouring from about 1853 but also issued in brown. Many moulded jugs were sold in sets, usually of three, although surviving sets of four or five are occasionally found.

Above left:
One of the earliest purely moulded jugs, by Phillips & Bagster of Hanley, c. 1818–23. Although the jug is apparently unmarked, the maker's name and address appear on dog collars in the main design and on the handle.

Above:
A popular jug published early in 1840 by William Ridgway, Son & Company of Hanley. The jousting knights were inspired by a medieval-style tournament held in August 1839 by the Earl of Eglinton at his castle in Ayrshire; it was the society event of the year, but sadly was marred by torrential rain.

From 1840 onwards relief-moulded jugs were a staple product for most potters making utilitarian wares. Among the more notable manufacturers was Samuel Alcock & Company, who made some fine jugs using a distinctive lavender colouring from about 1842 onwards. The well-known Copeland firm made a large number of designs, although few are of any real distinction, and two other prolific manufacturers were William Brownfield, in production from about 1850, and James Dudson. Brownfield made a large number of different designs, usually allocated titles such as 'Tyrol', 'Nile', 'Union' and very many others. James Dudson has already been noted for his manufacture of sprigged tankard-shaped jugs in the second half of the nineteenth century, but he also made a wide range of utilitarian moulded jugs, mostly with a bulbous body, wide upwards-flaring spout, and a simple strap or loop handle. Few of them are of any great merit, but in their day they were workmanlike, practical, and presumably deliberately aimed at the mass market. In view of the number that have survived, they must have been produced in very large quantities.

The designers of these jugs were not slow to realise the decorative potential of the technique, and they seem to have made jugs decorated with every subject imaginable. These include hunting scenes, Classical figures, mythical gods and goddesses, religious figures and biblical stories, scenes from

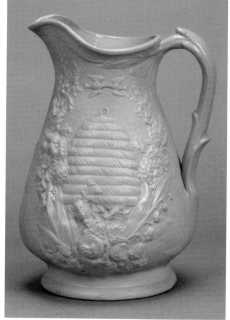

This jug depicting Silenus supported by satyrs (right) and the infant Bacchus riding on a donkey (left) was introduced by Minton but copied by other firms, including Mason and Stephen Green of Lambeth. Minton examples like these are of uniformly high quality but are more usually found in a pastel grey-green.

everyday life, and flora and fauna of every type. Commemorative designs were also made, but they tend to show all the signs of being rushed into production, generally being unmarked and of poor quality. Despite this, they are obviously popular with commemorative collectors and tend to fetch high prices.

Popular 'Naomi and Her Daughters-in-law' jugs, registered in 1847 by Samuel Alcock & Company, based on a painting by Henry Nelson O'Neill – also used for a Parian figure group by Minton. This distinctive lavender colour was favoured by Alcock, sometimes with the relief picked out, sometimes with the background coloured.

A fine green stoneware jug known as 'Three Soldiers', published in 1855 by Ridgway & Abington. The design commemorates the Crimean War and features the death of the Russian eagle. The small holes in the rim indicate a missing metal lid.

29

A jug by an unknown maker, c. 1830, depicting Robert Burns's characters Tam o' Shanter (right) and his friend Souter Johnnie (left). The high-relief figures are copied from sculptures by James Thom, now housed in a special statue house at the Burns Monument, Alloway, Ayrshire.

Few of the designs used by the potters were original and the vast majority were copied from prints that appeared in publications of the period. Many of the jugs were designed for the popular market, and illustrations from best-selling books were an obvious source for the potters. Examples from novels include *Paul and Virginia*, originally written in French by Bernadin de St Pierre but translated into English in 1795 by Helen Maria Williams, and *Uncle Tom's Cabin* by Harriet Beecher Stowe. More academic books were also used, such as Layard's story of his archaeological discoveries at Nineveh and Murphy's description of the palace at Alhambra. Other jugs based on engravings in books include the traditional ceremony of the Dunmow Flitch and Sir Sidney Smith's involvement in the Battle of Acre. Other subjects were taken from poems such as 'John Gilpin' by William Cowper, and 'Tam o' Shanter' and 'Willie Brew'd a Peck o' Maut', both by Robert Burns. Some jugs that

Three typical mid-nineteenth-century jugs with coloured backgrounds, featuring Cleopatra's Needle by Bradbury, Anderson & Bettany; a scenic design by T. J. & J. Mayer based on the popular novel *Paul and Virginia*; and a biblical design depicting David and Goliath by Thomas Till & Son.

survive in reasonable numbers are based on paintings by masters such as Rubens and Poussin, and by lesser but still noted artists such as John Singleton Copley, Thomas Stothard and Henry Nelson O'Neill. All of these would have been copied from engravings that appeared in periodicals such as the *Art Journal*, and not from the original paintings.

The potters made much use of the Design Registry system in an attempt to protect their designs from being copied, although this was not entirely successful and a number of copies can be found. However, many jugs are marked with the distinctive diamond-shaped registration symbol, which can be used both to identify the potter and to date the design. Marks are much more common on these mid-Victorian moulded jugs than on the earlier printed wares, and it tends to be the poorer-quality wares that are unmarked. The relatively large number of marked jugs makes their study particularly rewarding.

When the technique first appeared around 1820 some designs were enhanced with sprigging, particularly around the neck, a hangover from the earlier sprigged jugs described previously, but this practice soon died out. The earlier jugs were usually made in a single-colour stoneware, with buff being particularly popular, although white, grey and green are quite common. Blue was a little less popular. Some firms used distinctive colours, one example being a dark green used only by Minton. The plain jugs can be a little dull, and from the 1840s many potters enhanced the designs, initially with coloured backgrounds, but later with the moulding picked out with colour and sometimes added gilding. Eventually some quite garish jugs were made.

Relief-moulded jugs were produced in quantity throughout the nineteenth century, although the quality declined steadily after 1860 or so. Production clearly tailed off in the later years, probably in favour of other more decorative wares. Several early designs are being reproduced today, particularly by the Portmeirion Pottery, which rediscovered some old moulds and put them back into production. These jugs are stocked in many china shops today and are deservedly proving popular. They utilise a distinctive new body and are also clearly marked, so they are unlikely to confuse collectors seeking the original jugs.

A fine jug published in September 1841 by Wood & Brownfield of Cobridge, depicting King James I in the guise of the Judgement of Solomon, copied from a painting by Rubens, part of a famous set decorating the ceiling of the Banqueting House in Whitehall.

OTHER NINETEENTH-CENTURY JUGS

WHILE the three main techniques described above, or combinations of them, account for the majority of utilitarian jugs produced in the nineteenth century, several others were used. One of the earliest forms of decoration on pottery was painting, and hand-painted jugs were made throughout the period. Some of the most attractive are creamwares decorated with flamboyant flowers in overglaze enamels, made towards the end of the eighteenth century, particularly in Yorkshire and Staffordshire, but creamware had largely been superseded by pearlware by the turn of the century. Colourful floral painting on creamware survived longer in Bristol than elsewhere, mainly associated with a decorator called William Fifield.

In the early nineteenth century some decorative hand-painted jugs were still being made, but transfer printing had become the norm and painting was more widely used for special presentation pieces, jugs being particularly suitable. Many of these presentation jugs are dated and, with names and places often included in an inscription, it is sometimes possible to trace their history. They usually relate to births, marriages, deaths or similar family occasions, but occupational subjects such as industry, farming, coaching or carting, inns and public houses can be found.

Hand painting did still have a place for higher-quality jugs, particularly expensive porcelains, but also for the better earthenwares made by Spode, Wedgwood and some other quality manufacturers. Apart from the separate development of colouring over a printed outline, discussed a little later, hand painting steadily declined to rather gaudy splashes of colour, often applied by child labour rather than skilled decorators. This developed into a style known as either Gaudy Welsh or Gaudy Dutch, both misnomers since such wares were also made in quantity in Staffordshire. Examples tend to be of notably poor quality although from a distance they can look quite decorative. As a general rule, they date from the second half of the nineteenth century but earlier dated examples are known.

While hand painting was declining, the use of transfer printing expanded dramatically and the technique was used in various ways. Apart from printing

Opposite:
A fine Doulton Boer War jug commemorating Lord Roberts entering Pretoria and raising the flag on 5 June 1900.

Right:
A high-quality white earthenware jug with engine-turning around the base, hand painted in sepia with a wagoning scene. The front is inscribed for John Cash, the reverse with a verse, 'Such a Waggoner as Me ...', c. 1810.

Far right:
A high-quality Wedgwood black basalt jug of 'Club' shape, decorated with flower sprays in encaustic enamels, c. 1820.

on standard white wares, discussed earlier, there was a short period when a few manufacturers made jugs, and fewer mugs, printed overglaze in yellow on a brown body. These are very distinctive, often with chinoiserie or Paisley-style floral patterns, either of which can be found with Nelson commemorative medallions let into the main design.

Printing can also be found on yellow-bodied jugs and on pearlware jugs where the main decoration is lustre colouring. Lustre first appeared at the beginning of the nineteenth century, initially a silver colour, actually made using platinum, but later pink or copper, both produced using gold. Silver

A good pair of Swansea 'Cymro Stone China' pouch-shaped jugs, colourfully enamelled with flowers and with an inscription for Thomas and Joanna Burch of Winchester in Hampshire, dated 1838.

34

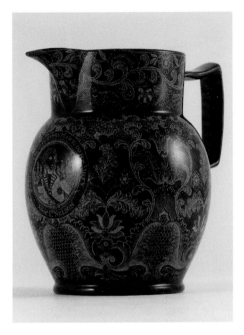

Top left:
A brown-bodied jug printed in yellow with a Paisley-type design incorporating a medallion portrait of Admiral Lord Nelson with his famous order 'England Expects Every Man To Do His Duty', c. 1806–10. The same Nelson medallion can be found on similar jugs with different backgrounds.

Top right:
An early nineteenth-century yellow-printed brown-bodied jug, this example with a Greek figure design more usually seen on blue-printed dinner wares.

Middle right:
A Gaudy Welsh jug, crudely painted and lustred but particularly early, with an inscription recording the death of eleven-year-old Martha Collier in 1829; the name Gaudy Welsh should not be taken literally since similar jugs were made in Staffordshire and elsewhere, usually later in the nineteenth century.

Bottom right:
A Dutch-shape jug covered with a canary-yellow glaze and printed with figural scenes featuring Hope and Charity, lined with silver lustre, c. 1810–20.

Above left: A Dutch-shape jug decorated overall in silver-resist lustre with scenic reserves printed in purple, c. 1810–20.

Above: An ornate copper lustre jug with oval reserves printed in purple and enamel-coloured with Adam Buck-type mother and child scenes, c. 1820–30.

Left: A fine pink lustre jug of Sunderland type, although this example was probably potted in Newcastle. The front is inscribed and dated 1839, and the lifeboat scene commemorates the famous rescue by Grace Darling and her father, William, of the crew from the steamer *Forfarshire*, which foundered on 7 September 1838.

lustre was often applied using a resist technique that could produce decorative patterns, often floral, but sometimes with exotic birds or other designs.

Copper lustre involved use of the gold on a dark background, often solid red clay, but also achieved by painting a brown background over which the lustre was applied. Early copper lustre jugs usually have printed patterns as part of the decoration, sometimes with added colouring, but later jugs were produced in quantity for the low end of the market, decorated overall with the lustre but overpainted with enamels, usually quite crudely, with flowers, scrolls or other simple designs.

Pink lustre is made with gold on a white background and was to become particularly associated with the potteries of Sunderland, although similar wares were also made in quantity at Newcastle upon Tyne. Pink lustre was also widely used in Staffordshire, although there it tended to be used for lining around rims and on handles, and also for framing printed panels, often applied in a matching non-lustre purple colour. Such wares were not made in the north-east, despite almost any use of pink lustre being described as 'Sunderland'. One other group of wares is hand-painted with naïve but rather attractive pink lustre landscapes, usually featuring cottages or churches. These were made in various pottery districts, including South Wales, but jugs are relatively uncommon.

On the other hand, pink lustre jugs from Sunderland and Newcastle are quite numerous and deservedly popular. The printed designs include religious and other verses, ships, hunting and genre scenes, and a large number of views of the famous iron bridge at Sunderland. They are bright and colourful and can often be attributed to specific potteries such as the Garrison Pottery in Sunderland or Maling from Newcastle.

Some of them were made as gifts and painted with inscriptions and dates. As with the earlier creamware and pearlware presentation jugs, they sometimes commemorate public dignitaries or significant local events although most were either presented to lesser folk such as businessmen, publicans and farmers, or were made for family occasions. These can be of great sentimental value when passed down as family heirlooms.

Pink lustre is also occasionally found on jugs as an overall wash covering black-printed designs, usually with pink lining around the rim and base. These all seem to be of Staffordshire origin, mostly made by one or two small firms, although marked Davenport examples are known.

One of the benefits of transfer printing was the ability to print an outline that could then be filled in by hand. This approach appeared early in the century on good-quality pearlware jugs, typical of the period, and there was also a relatively brief fashion in the 1820s for jugs printed in dark blue and highlighted with coloured enamels. These are often described as 'Opaque China' in the printed marks, although this phrase was widely used elsewhere.

Below left:
Another typical pink lustre jug, this example with a portrait of a sailor and his girl titled 'Susan & William', the front with a verse 'Here's to the Wind that Blows', the reverse bearing one of many prints of the famous iron bridge at Sunderland, c. 1840.

Below:
A rare Garrison Pottery lustre jug, hand painted with flags proclaiming 'No Monopoly' and 'No Impressment', c. 1820. The use of press gangs to recruit sailors strained relations between Britain and the United States in the early nineteenth century, with at least five thousand American citizens being taken.

Top left:
A 'Marble'-pattern jug by Everard, Colclough & Townsend of Lane End, sheet-printed in black and washed overall in pink lustre, c. 1840. This use of overall lustre does not appear to have been widely popular.

Top right:
A Dutch-shape jug of c. 1810–25, outline-printed in black with exotic birds and a rural scene, and extensively enamelled in colours.

Bottom left:
A fine-quality Spode 'Antique'-shape jug printed overall in 'pigmuck' green with the factory's 'Tumbledown Dick' pattern, picked out with enamel colours, c. 1820.

Bottom right:
A Mason's Patent Ironstone China jug of common octagonal 'Hydra' shape decorated with a typical Japanese-style pattern, c. 1820–30. This example is of relatively early date, but similar jugs were made in large quantities throughout the nineteenth century.

The addition of colour to these printed wares is often described as 'clobbering', although this term should strictly be reserved for printed wares that were not originally intended to be coloured. The printing and colouring technique was also used at major potteries for higher-quality wares, the best examples, not surprisingly, being made by Spode or Wedgwood.

Outline printing came to be particularly widely used on ironstone wares with so-called Japan patterns, made popular by the famous Mason firm but employed by both important and smaller, less prestigious potbanks of the period. Jugs with this type of decoration were made in very large numbers throughout the nineteenth century and, although often rather crudely decorated, they can be bright and attractive and are popular for decoration. The bodies used are various forms of stone china, which is tough and durable, especially suitable for hard-wearing utilitarian jugs. Printed marks often feature marketing trade names such as 'Opaque China', 'Granite Ware', 'Indian Ironstone', 'Oriental Stone', 'Pearl Stone Ware' and 'Improved Stone China', although there is little difference between them.

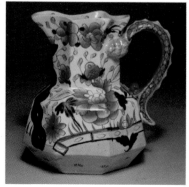

These colourful stone china jugs became a staple product for many of the potteries in the middle of the nineteenth century, but new products were needed to stimulate sales, and one of the most striking was majolica. This involved the application of coloured glazes on to moulded earthenwares and was named after the early Italian tin-glazed wares known as maiolica. In practice these new wares were very different from anything else then available, and for a period between 1850 and the mid 1880s they became hugely popular.

Top:
An attractive and good-quality Minton majolica jug moulded with overlapping lily leaves, marked with model number 1228 and an impressed date code for 1868.

Middle left:
A Wedgwood majolica jug decorated with a Shakespearean quote: 'What tho' my cates be poor, take them in good part, better cheer may you have, but not with better heart' – 'cates' being another word for food. This 'Caterer' jug was designed by Frederick Bret Russel and produced in twenty-one different colourways from 1867.

Middle right:
A fine and decorative majolica jug by George Jones, c. 1872. Jones originally worked for Minton but set up in Stoke in 1861 and produced some of the most esoteric and collectable majolica.

Bottom:
Three typical majolica jugs made at Hanley in Staffordshire in the 1870s; these are by James Dudson, Samuel Lear and Banks & Thorley, the last registered in 1876.

Below: A fine Doulton artist-decorated jug of tankard shape with a silver rim, incised with a scene of horses by Hannah Barlow, one of the most collectable of the Doulton artists.

Below right: One of a range of Doulton jugs decorated with mottoes and sayings. This example reads: 'Straight is the line of duty, curved is the line of beauty; follow the straight line thou shalt see, the curved line ever follow thee.' This is the most common shape but many others can be found.

The highest-quality wares were made by Wedgwood, Minton, Copeland and George Jones, but many of the smaller potteries also adopted the technique with varying degrees of success. The top-quality wares can be magnificent, whereas some of the lesser pieces are almost equally dreadful.

The only other major technique to be employed in making jugs is incised and carved decoration. Since these are hand processes, they require skilled labour and so they were not commonly used. However, towards the end of the century there was a movement back to hand craftsmanship, notable especially in the artist-decorated stonewares produced by the Doulton firm at Lambeth. This factory was one of several that produced brown salt-glazed stoneware, mainly utilitarian pieces such as bottles and jars, architectural items for the building trade, and even drainpipes. The output did include moulded and sprigged wares but, because of the nature of the brown body, these were fairly crude in comparison with the finer wares discussed above. Many jugs in two-tone brown stoneware with white sprigged ornament were made by Doulton and other London makers, but also at Bristol and in Derbyshire and elsewhere. They are often referred to today as hunting jugs, reflecting the subjects most often used for the sprigging, rather than their use.

Starting in about 1870, Doulton set up a studio to produce stonewares decorated by a group of artists and assistants. These wares proved highly popular, and some of the main artists, such as Hannah, Florence and Arthur Barlow, George Tinworth and Mark Marshall, achieved considerable distinction. Many of the junior artists and assistants also produced attractive

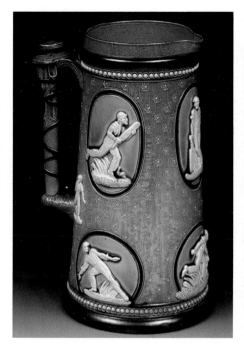 

wares, and some of the more straightforward designs were put into production. Although many jugs came to be made, the better artist wares were intended to be decorative and not really for everyday use. Some of the simpler versions were produced for more utilitarian usage, among which is an attractive range decorated with short verses or sayings, such as 'Bread at pleasure, drink by measure' or 'Bitter must be the cup that a smile will not sweeten'. These were introduced in the 1880s, initially made by some of the main artists with the inscriptions and other decoration sprigged in coloured clays, but the more popular versions were later simplified for mass production, with the inscriptions impressed or printed rather than sprigged.

Various other Doulton jugs are found, among which are some decorated with sporting subjects such as rugby, cycling or golf, the last being much sought after today. There is also a range of jugs commemorating people or events, including Gladstone, Disraeli, Queen Victoria and the Boer War.

Other art potters produced jugs at a similar period, including well-known names such as the Martin Brothers, William de Morgan and William Moorcroft, but their wares were almost always predominantly decorative in nature, and they were the forerunners of the studio pottery movement that was to emerge in the twentieth century.

Above left:
A Doulton Lambeth stoneware jug decorated with cricketing vignettes. Note the handle moulded as a group of bats, balls and boots under a straw boater, c. 1881.

Above:
A Martinware stoneware jug signed and dated 1880. The pottery is more widely known for the grotesque bird pots and face jugs made by Robert Wallace Martin.

NOVELTY JUGS

THE POTTERY INDUSTRY, like many others, was hard on its workers, who had to endure poor and often dangerous working conditions. But this did not prevent them from exhibiting a good sense of humour, which can be seen in the range of novelty wares that were produced.

These are typified particularly by the well-known Toby jug, which first appeared towards the end of the eighteenth century, although its development came alongside other jugs moulded with figural characteristics. Examples include jugs moulded as heads or with faces beneath the spout, some with correspondingly ornate handles and spouts.

The Toby jug itself depicts a fat, rather jovial toper, seated with a jug of ale and a pipe, although many other versions were made over the years. Most are in earthenware, and the early creamware and pearlware examples with translucent coloured glazes are particularly sought after. Later examples are decorated with coloured enamels and, while some are of high quality, many are relatively poor. This is particularly true of twentieth-century examples, although a very fine set was made by the Wilkinson firm depicting leaders in the First World War.

Unlike other jugs, the Toby was made primarily as an ornament, produced alongside figures and other decorative wares. It was never intended as a utilitarian vessel, and as a result it tends to appeal to specialists rather than general jug collectors. The same is true of another novelty jug – the cow creamer – which is moulded as a complete cow, its tail curved to form a handle, its mouth acting as a spout, and with a small covered hole in its back for filling. The best examples come from the early nineteenth century, made in Staffordshire or Yorkshire, but later examples of lesser quality can be found. Some even have their bodies rather inappropriately printed in blue with the 'Willow' pattern.

The stoneware potters of London, Derbyshire and elsewhere also produced moulded figural wares, Doulton & Watts and Stephen Green, for example, making jugs moulded as Nelson and Wellington. Stoneware jugs are also quite common moulded as caricature heads, mainly just humorous rather than lampooning specific people. These caricatures, together with

Opposite:
A fine moulded and colourfully enamelled Satyr jug by Shorthose of Hanley, inscribed and dated 1819. It is rare to find jugs of this type and period with any maker's mark.

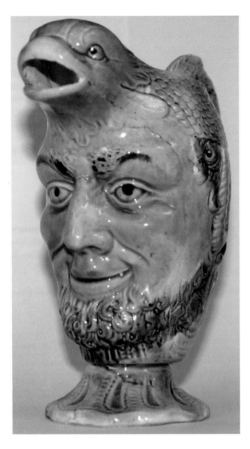

Above left:
A small eighteenth-century novelty jug, possibly by Ralph Wood, moulded in the form of Neptune's head surmounted by a dolphin, whose tail forms the handle, all covered with coloured glazes.

Above right:
A brown salt-glazed stoneware jug by Doulton & Watts of Lambeth, moulded as Admiral Lord Nelson, the foot inscribed 'Trafalgar 1805'. Nelson commemoratives were made for many years after the famous sea battle and this example probably dates from about 1830.

Right:
A typical mid-nineteenth-century brown salt-glazed stoneware caricature jug, in this case a man wearing a nightcap with its tip forming the spout. Face jugs of this general type are not uncommon.

Top left:
An early nineteenth-century Toby jug of traditional shape, enamelled in colours. Eighteenth-century examples are normally covered with coloured glazes.

Top right:
A Toby jug of traditional shape, sparsely decorated in underglaze blue, c. 1820.

Two Wilkinson jugs of Toby type, from a set of eleven designed by Sir Francis Carruthers Gould depicting First World War leaders. These represent Earl Kitchener of Khartoum (his jug inscribed 'Bitter for the Kaiser') and Marshall Foch (his bottle inscribed 'Au diable le Kaiser'), c. 1915–20.

45

Right: A pearlware cow creamer decorated with sponged and painted Pratt-type colours, possibly Yorkshire, c. 1820. This is a typical model although the bases vary considerably and the milkmaid is not always present.

Below: A delftware or tin-glazed earthenware puzzle jug, probably potted in either Liverpool or London, decorated with a traditional verse, 'Here Gentlemen come try y'skill …', c. 1750–60.

popular Toby jugs, can be seen as the forerunners of the more recent fashion for character jugs produced by Doulton and others, very popular with modern collectors but never intended to be used as jugs.

There is one other form of novelty jug that was intended for use, albeit in rather special circumstances. The puzzle jug can be traced back many years, both in Britain and on the Continent, particularly in Italy. It consists of a jug vessel with a neck that is pierced but has the normal pouring spout replaced by a rim fitted with several protruding tube-like spouts. With the pierced neck it is impossible to pour the contents normally, but the trick is that the spouts around the rim are connected to a hollow handle. Thus, by covering all but one of the spouts, the liquid can be sucked up through the remaining spout. However, this might be a little too easy, so the potters positioned an extra air hole, usually up underneath the handle, which needed to be covered before the contents could be drunk. With modern health and safety legislation, it is unlikely that such jugs would be allowed today.

Puzzle jugs first appeared in widespread production in tin-glazed earthenware or delftware towards the end of the seventeenth century and became very popular. Most are decorated with an inscription along the lines of:

Come gentlemen and try your skill
I'll hold a wager if you will
That you can't drink this liquor all
Unless you spill or let some fall.

There are very many variants of this traditional rhyme, and one favourite of the author is:

In this can there is good liquor
Fit for parson or for vicar
But how to drink and not to spill
Will try the utmost of your skill.

The enduring popularity of the puzzle jug can be inferred from their production throughout successive centuries. In the eighteenth century the delftware body was superseded by creamware and then pearlware, both of which continued into the nineteenth century, to be joined by ordinary earthenwares and brown salt-glazed stoneware. Puzzle jugs became popular with country potters in areas such as Devon, where slipwares continued to be made up to modern times.

The use of verses on puzzle jugs was less dominant in the nineteenth century, when more standard painted or transfer-printed decoration became the norm. They were always popular for presentation, and inscribed and dated examples are not uncommon. The basic form remained unchanged, although there are many different body shapes and the number of spouts can vary. Jugs are known with a single spout while one has been recorded with as many as seven, requiring a real contortionist to extract the contents. A few examples were made at Swansea with dummy spouts and extra holes irregularly hidden around the body, making usage even more of a challenge.

There is one other form of puzzle jug that is less well known. This looks like a normal jug but has a hole in the base and is fitted with an internal tube, which, allied to a hole under the hollow handle, can be used to siphon liquid ready to spill on an unsuspecting victim. These were made in quite large numbers in the 1850s and 1860s by Elsmore & Forster of Tunstall, usually printed with designs including cock-fighting or Grimaldi the clown, but others can be found with relief-moulded decoration and by different makers.

Below:
A fine pearlware puzzle jug, possibly from Yorkshire, decorated in underglaze blue with a hand-painted scene of two men smoking and drinking at a tripod table, which bears a bowl and two glasses and also a puzzling number, '666', c. 1790.

Below:
A rather late creamware puzzle jug, possibly from Yorkshire or Bristol, attractively enamelled in colours and inscribed 'Samuel Mellor, 1825'.

Left:
A dated puzzle jug in salt-glazed brown stoneware, probably from Nottingham or Derbyshire, inscribed 'Wm & Hannah Hallam, Noseley, Leicestershire 1866'.

Bottom left:
A Swansea puzzle jug of pouch shape, colourfully enamelled with flowers, c. 1835–40. This jug has dummy spouts and extra erratically spaced holes hidden beneath the brown lining.

Below:
An Elsmore & Forster puzzle jug of siphon type, printed and coloured with Harlequin and cock-fighting scenes, c. 1860. Similar examples often feature Grimaldi the clown. Note the small hole inside the top of the handle.

THE TWENTIETH
CENTURY

A T THE TURN of the century there was no great change in jug production, just the usual steady developments in design and technical improvements. However, one of the most notable new designs was a range known as 'series ware' produced by Doulton, not alongside their stonewares made in Lambeth but at a Staffordshire pottery taken over from Pinder, Bourne & Company in 1882.

Series ware was introduced towards the end of the nineteenth century by Charles Noke, the firm's art director, but it was in the early 1900s that it blossomed. The wares were colour-printed with a large number of different designs based on literature, history, sport, and particularly popular imagery and rural England. The range was vast and production continued, albeit curtailed by the Second World War, until the 1960s. Series ware jugs are distinctive, with the firm deliberately developing new shapes. There were also related ranges, some with moulded decoration, such as Kingsware, with figures on a highly glazed brown ground.

While Doulton's series ware was generally colourful and cheerful, there was a particularly dramatic change in popular pottery in the 1920s following the horrors of the First World War. This was Art Deco, inspired by the Paris Exhibition of 1925, and the new bright, even garish, and angular styles were a revelation. They are particularly associated with Clarice Cliff, although two other female ceramic artists, Charlotte Rhead and Susie Cooper, also came to prominence.

Clarice Cliff spent most of her working life at the Royal Staffordshire Pottery (and the adjoining Newport Pottery) of Arthur Wilkinson in Burslem. Her 'Bizarre' range, initially of abstract geometric designs, was introduced in 1928 and was instantly successful. Floral patterns, including the popular 'Crocus' design, followed, and many more joined the range in the 1930s. Most of them are to be found on jugs, for which several distinctive shapes were developed, including a large Lotus jug. Clarice Cliff became known as the 'Sunshine Girl', and her wares are hugely popular today.

A Royal Doulton series ware jug, one of a very wide range produced at Burslem in Staffordshire. This example is decorated with 'Dr Johnson at the Cheshire Cheese', c. 1920.

Above: A Royal Doulton jug from Burslem, a limited edition 'Dickens jug' shown with its original certificate. Although not strictly series ware, these moulded pieces are closely related.

Left: A Clarice Cliff 'Bizarre' range jug of so-called 'Athens' shape, number 36, decorated with one of the particularly popular 'Crocus' patterns, in production from 1928 right through to 1963.

Opposite page top: A small but very colourful Clarice Cliff 'Bizarre' series jug of shape number 564 (known as 'George'), decorated with the 'Nasturtium' pattern, c. 1930–5.

Opposite bottom left: A fine and large Clarice Cliff 'Lotus' jug decorated with a 'Bizarre' pattern from the 'Fantasque' range known as 'Blue Chintz', introduced c. 1933.

Opposite bottom right: A typical Charlotte Rhead jug with tube-lined and gilt decoration on shape number 250, c. 1935.

Of the other two renowned women potters, Charlotte Rhead made some fine jugs decorated with a tube-lining technique, particularly in the 'Crown Ducal' range produced during her time with A. G. Richardson. Larger serving jugs from Susie Cooper are somewhat less common, as her output concentrated on tablewares.

Several other firms produced interesting jugs in the 1930s, and names to look out for include Carlton Ware (made by Wiltshaw & Robinson of Stoke), Shelley (the name initiated by Wileman & Company, who developed into Shelley Potteries Ltd) and Burleigh Ware (from Burgess & Leigh of Burslem). Two other firms of interest are Wade, Heath & Company of Burslem (who made some unusual Art Deco shapes)

Left:
A large Carlton Ware jug in the firm's popular 'Oak Tree' pattern from the 1930s. This example is the daytime version with beige background; a night-time version has a grey-blue ground.

Below left:
A simple but attractive Shelley jug decorated only with ribbed colour banding.

Below:
A Fielding's Crown Devon jug made to commemorate the aborted coronation of Edward VIII in 1937. Fielding's made a range of moulded and coloured jugs in this style, some of which are fitted with small musical movements activated when the jug is lifted.

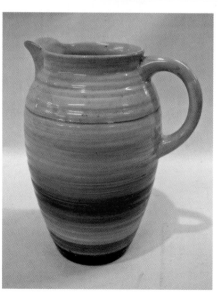

and Myott, Son & Company of Cobridge, whose jugs are not of the highest quality but are bright and decorative.

One other Staffordshire firm to note is S. Fielding & Company of Stoke, who made a wide range of jugs using their Crown Devon trade name. Among them are moulded and brightly coloured jugs, often fitted with appropriate musical movements, featuring such tunes as 'John Peel', 'Daisy Bell', 'Ilkley Moor', 'Widdicombe Fair' and the songs of Harry Lauder.

The Poole Pottery, at Poole in Dorset, started life as Carter & Company in 1873, producing architectural pottery, and became Carter, Stabler & Adams in 1921 before finally adopting the name 'Poole Pottery' in 1963. Decorative wares were introduced early in the century and the firm went on to develop a fine range of hand-decorated ceramics. The firm being based well away from any other pottery centres, the wares became quite distinctive and many fine jugs were made. A range of colourful traditional patterns, mostly floral based, was introduced in the 1930s and is particularly popular. It remained in production long after the Second World War but other innovative styles have been made since, although jugs are less common, with a preponderance of vases and various flatwares.

With the steady decline in the use of serving jugs, opportunities for collectors are much reduced. Where jugs are to be found in china shops, they are usually seen as decorative rather than functional, more likely to be used for displaying flowers than pouring milk or ale. We have to wonder what the twenty-first century will bring.

A typically colourful Poole Pottery jug in shape number 309, decorated with one of the factory's traditional patterns from the 1950s.

PLACES TO VISIT

Allen Gallery, Church Street, Alton, Hampshire, GU34 2BW. A small but high-quality ceramics gallery. Telephone: 0845 603 5635.
Website: www3.hants.gov.uk/museum/allen-gallery

Brighton Museum and Art Gallery, Royal Pavilion Gardens, Brighton, East Sussex, BN1 1EE. A fine department of ceramics, especially the Willett collection of commemorative pottery. Telephone: 01273 292882.
Website: www.brighton.virtualmuseum.info

Bristol City Museum and Art Gallery, Queen's Road, Bristol, BS8 1RL. An informative display of Bristol pottery and porcelain.
Telephone: 0117 922 3571. Website: www.bristol.gov.uk/museums

National Museum of Wales, Cathays Park, Cardiff, CF10 3NP. A definitive collection featuring the Morton Nance Collection of Welsh Pottery and Porcelain. Telephone: 029 2039 7951.
Website: www.museumwales.ac.uk/en/cardiff

Victoria and Albert Museum, Cromwell Road, South Kensington, London, SW7 2RL. A vast display of ceramics including jugs of all types. At the time of writing the ceramics galleries were closed for major refurbishment with partial reopening scheduled for September 2009 and completion in 2010.
Telephone: 020 7942 2000. Website: www.vam.ac.uk

Salisbury and South Wiltshire Museum, The King's House, 65 The Close, Salisbury, Wiltshire, SP1 2EN. A small ceramics gallery with several interesting jugs and an excellent collection of Wedgwood pottery.
Telephone: 01722 332151. Website: www.salisburymuseum.org.uk

The Potteries Museum and Art Gallery, Bethesda Street, Hanley, Stoke-on-Trent, Staffordshire, ST1 3DW. Britain's foremost ceramics museum in the heart of the Staffordshire Potteries. Telephone: 01782 232323.
Website: www.stoke.gov.uk/ccm/navigation/leisure/museums

Sunderland Museum and Winter Gardens, Burdon Road, Sunderland, SR1 1PP. The world's largest collection of Sunderland pottery with fine examples of pink lustre jugs. Telephone: 0191 553 2323.
Website: www.twmuseums.org.uk/sunderland

Glynn Vivian Art Gallery, Alexandra Road, Swansea, SA1 5DZ. A good collection of local Swansea pottery and porcelain. Telephone: 01792 516900. Website: www.swansea.gov.uk/index.cfm?articleid=1394

BIBLIOGRAPHY

Coysh, A. W., and Henrywood, R.K. *The Dictionary of Blue and White Printed Pottery 1780–1880* (two volumes). Antique Collectors' Club, Woodbridge, 1982 and 1989.

Gibson, Michael. *19th Century Lustreware*. Antique Collectors' Club, Woodbridge, 1999.

Godden, G. A. *British Pottery, an Illustrated Guide*. Barrie & Jenkins, London, 1974.

Godden, G. A., and Gibson, M. *Collecting Lustreware*. Barrie & Jenkins, London, 1991.

Henrywood, R. K. *Relief-Moulded Jugs 1820–1900*. Antique Collectors' Club, Woodbridge, 1984.

Henrywood, R. K. *An Illustrated Guide to British Jugs*. Swan Hill Press, Shrewsbury, 1997.

Hughes, Kathy. *A Collector's Guide to Nineteenth-Century Jugs* (two volumes). Routledge & Kegan Paul, London and Boston, 1985, and Taylor Publishing Company, Dallas, 1991.

Lewis, Griselda. *A Collector's History of English Pottery*. Antique Collectors' Club, Woodbridge, 1987.

Lewis, Griselda. *Pratt Ware – English and Scottish Relief Decorated and Underglaze Coloured Earthenware, 1780–1840*. Antique Collectors' Club, Woodbridge, 2006.

Northern Ceramics Society. *Stonewares & Stone Chinas of Northern England to 1851* (exhibition catalogue). City Museum & Art Gallery, Stoke-on-Trent, 1982.

Paton, James. *Jugs – A Collector's Guide*. Souvenir Press, London, 1976.

Rumsey, Jill. *Victorian Relief-Moulded Jugs*. Richard Dennis, London, 1987.

INDEX

Figures in *italics* refer to illustrations